THE
INNER
COMPASS

THE
INNER
COMPASS

Cultivating
the Courage
to Trust Yourself

LAWRENCE YEO

CONTENTS

INTRODUCTION
WHAT THIS BOOK IS ABOUT

As a service to your attention, this book is short. In roughly 100 pages, I will detail why self-understanding is the solution to suffering, and how you can import this sentiment into daily life. Because if you do the work to look within, you'll find that external circumstances may jolt you, but they'll never derail you.

I've written this book for two reasons:

1. An earlier version of myself would have benefited from its existence, and
2. Your present self can avoid the pain that my prior self once experienced.

Here's the thing. Throughout most of my youth and early adulthood, I believed that external achievements would alleviate my inner turmoils. If I wasn't at peace, I figured that there was some ambition I needed to actualize, or some milestone I had to reach to justify a period of ease. In my mind, peace was not a given. It had to be earned, over and over again.

This, of course, is a false belief, but it's one thing to *know* it and a whole other thing to *understand* it. Knowledge is taught through information, but understanding is taught through experience. So while you may rationally know that external outcomes aren't the answer, your daily experience may indicate otherwise. Chances are, you'll continue chasing prestige, success, and approval because you're conditioned to do so, and it's only after decades of this pursuit where you accumulate enough experience to see through the illusoriness of it all.

The goal of this book is to bridge the gap between

knowledge and understanding, and to do it succinctly. It's to take the essence of what would have taken years to personally experience, and to distill it down to 100 pages that act as an expressway to insight. By the end of this book, you'll be equipped with the mental tools to strengthen your resolve, and to trust in the unique voice that is your intuition.

This is important because each day, our resolve is tested. We live in a world where people are incentivized to disturb the stillness within us, usually by making us feel inadequate or alone. Social media feeds, for example, are nothing more than engineered highlight reels that generate envy, all of which we subject ourselves to in the name of entertainment. It's no surprise that we outsource our judgments to others, given that we rarely take the time to examine the depths of our own minds.

This book is a call to reverse the tide and have it gravitate back toward the inner domain. There is no force greater than the confirmation you give yourself, as it's the only lasting avenue to contentment. All external praise or criticism—no matter how important it feels in the moment—quickly fades into the crevices of the mind. The only thing that lasts is the labyrinth of your inner world, and like anything worthwhile, it takes effort to navigate and understand.

So in the name of understanding, we take our first step into the unknown. And in doing so, we commit to the end goal of trusting ourselves, regardless of what any other voice may say.

THE
INNER
COMPASS

CHAPTER 1
THE SEARCH FOR PEACE

DEPRESSION ISN'T FEELING DOWN when things are going badly. It's feeling down even when things are going well.

I know this because in my twenties, I stared into the abyss for a prolonged period of time. Despite having a roof over my head, food in my stomach, and loved ones who cared for me, I couldn't shake the feeling that something was terribly wrong. There was a gap between the reality of my biological safety and the contents of my psychological distress, and it was growing into a chasm with each passing day.

It's hard to describe what depression is to someone who hasn't experienced it, let alone someone who has. The most difficult thing about depression is the belief in its specificity; that the kind you have is wholly unique to you. This makes you believe that no one can comprehend what you're experiencing, which further deepens the depths of your despair. Oftentimes, loneliness has little to do with the lack of people around you, but the lack of people who understand you.

This leads to a retreat into one's own thoughts, much of which has been corrupted by self-loathing. If you truly believe that no one can understand you, then you begin to question why exactly people love you.

Are they obligated to do so? What have I done to deserve it? Why love me when there are so many other people out there that are more worthy of it?

If these questions sound absurd to you, that's because they are. But when your mind is in a dark place, it attempts to justify that darkness through the vehicle of deception. It will take any source of light and dim it so it can no longer be found. This is how recipients of love can feel unloved, and how providers of acceptance can feel unaccepted. The mind creates narratives that serve whatever condition it's in, and the darker its state, the darker its stories.

Now, as I stated in the introduction, there is a difference between knowledge and understanding. When I was depressed, I *knew* that my mind was on a faulty operating system, dispensing lies about the state of my life. I knew that my family loved me, that I was worthy of it, and that I had so much to give. But I couldn't *understand* it because of the stories that were circulating in my mind. The stories of self-deprecation and shame were too convincing, and I thought that I needed to prove myself over and over again (via achievements or ambitions) to quiet the volume of those tales.

Well, here's the good news. Knowledge can

become understanding when you least expect it, and it can strike you at a moment's notice. It can take the form of an experience you have, a conversation with a friend, or a serendipitous insight that sticks.

In my case, the journey into understanding—and out of depression—all started with a single question:

66 *Who created these stories I'm telling myself?*

That's it. No avalanche of insight. No punch of profundity. Just a simple question that arose on a random day.

The powerful thing about questions, however, is that they're the birthplace of answers. This sounds painfully obvious, but everything about the world indicates that people don't see this connection. Political discourse, for example, is a steady stream of opinions about what must be right, but no inquiries about what may be missing.

This is where the art of asking questions comes in.

When you're able to sit with a question and commit to understanding it, then you'll see things that were once veiled from view. You'll look beyond generalizations and see the many pieces that are required to form the basis of a lasting answer.

Usually the answer is simple, but it takes an effortful framing of the initial question to understand the simplicity of the response.

So when this question arose, I could have ignored it, but something told me to sit with it and explore it further. Something told me to follow it, to see where it leads.

Well, as it turns out, this search changed the course of my life.

And by diving into it together, it just might change yours too.

CHAPTER 2
THE SOURCE OF SUFFERING

FOR BETTER OR FOR WORSE, the oldest stories endure.

The reason why religious texts hold so much power isn't merely due to their content, but also their age. If these same texts were published for the first time today, they not only would sound trite, they would probably sound crazy. It matters that the source material dates back a few millennia, as many generations imbued it with the meaning required for it to compound into what it is today.

The same goes for economics, technology, and even culture. Fads come and go, but the influences that generate them remain the same. As they say, everything is a remix, which means that the original source material finds its way through it all.

We give old stories a tremendous amount of relevance. And while this seems obvious at larger scales, what we often miss is that it's just as true at the smallest scale:

At the level of the self.

When you think about the trajectory of your life, what is the origin point of all the narratives? What's the one period in your life that gives significance to all the others?

I'm sure that many important things have happened to you in the last year or so, but I'm guessing that none of them are the answer.

That's because the most significant part of life, regardless of who you are, is your upbringing. Even if you don't remember too much from it, the little you do has an outsized impact on your worldview because they're the oldest stories you carry. Your most formative years hold incredible weight in how you craft the narrative of your life.

In the last chapter, I outlined the question that began my journey:

66 *Who created these stories I'm telling myself?*

Although it seemed to randomly appear in my mind, I realized that it arose because things weren't adding up. I had the benefit of a happy childhood, so the dark stories of shame and self-sabotage couldn't have come from my parents. I also couldn't point to any single event from my upbringing that would act as invisible line to the depression I felt as an adult.

So then I asked if I created these stories myself, but that didn't make sense either. Why would anyone willingly manufacture lies about how worthless they may be? If you had the choice between contentment and despair, no one in their right mind would choose the latter. It just didn't make sense.

This conundrum baffled me until one day, my parents showed me a photo album of my childhood years. As they flipped through each page, I couldn't help but to notice how my eyes contained so much joy and ease in each captured moment. When I asked my mom if she carefully selected these photos to showcase, she shook her head and said, "No, you were always like this. In fact, your nickname was 'Happy Boy.'"

There are special moments when someone's words become your epiphanies, even if the speaker had no intention of delivering them.

This was one of those moments for me.

Two questions immediately came to mind:

If happiness was my baseline, how could depression be a natural descendant of it? What had to intervene so that my innate source of light would go on to produce so much darkness?

Fortunately, as soon as these questions emerged, the answer did as well.

What I understood then was that contentment is our default condition, but it is constantly disturbed by external pressures, either subtle or direct. If we are born with the attribute of presence, then anything that takes us away from it can't be a product of our own making.

Any doubts or fears we have about ourselves are not created from within, but rather by an external force that has convinced us of its truth. This force is called **conditioning**, which is the source of all tension and suffering we feel.

You'll notice that I said conditioning can be subtle or direct. The direct forms of conditioning are more obvious and acute in nature, such as a bad childhood or a traumatic event. These are steep troughs in experience that you can readily identify, and you can target them as specific sources of turmoil.

The subtle forms of conditioning, on the other hand, aren't as obvious but just as present. They take the form of expectations, norms, judgments, status, and other influences that divide and organize people into hierarchical structures. While they don't generate shocks like traumatic events do, they gradually erode your contentment until none of it remains.

Regardless of the type of conditioning, both are external in nature, and both are effective in diminishing your resolve. At its core, that's what suffering is. It's the belief that peace can't be found within yourself, so you have to attain it through a series of outcomes. This is why the Buddha famously linked desire with suffering, knowing that desire always required an external goal or objective to be satisfied.

The problem, however, is that conditioning has been an omnipresent force in our lives, dating all the way back to the first year of existence. We've always looked outward to validate our sense of safety, starting with our parents and then into society at large.

There's a fascinating concept called social referencing that helps illustrate this point. In short, when we are babies, we use our mother's emotional state as a map to navigate our physical world. So if a baby is crawling around a sofa and sees a short drop, he'll first look to his mother to get a sense of her reaction. If she's anxious, he will absorb that anxiety and exercise caution. But if she's calm and collected, he will adopt that state and proceed onward. This happens at a moment's notice, without any conscious thought.

As this baby grows older, he will develop more autonomy from his mother, but this pattern of looking outward to regulate his inner state will continue. What it means to be educated, what it means to be successful, and what it means to have influence will all depend on how others judge and perceive him. And given that people favorably judge that which they already know, he will be incentivized to imitate the familiar.

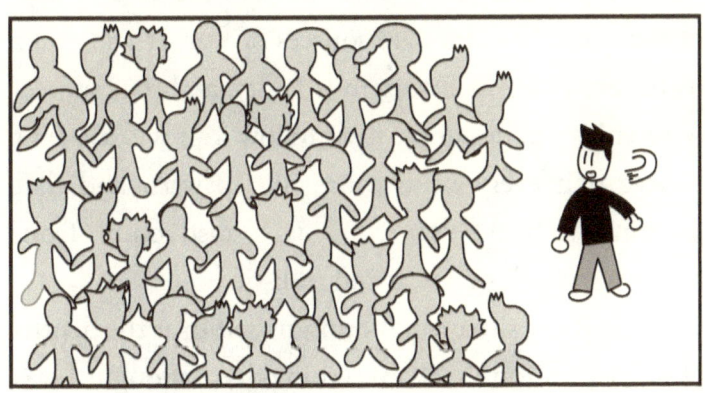

While this may lead to money and accolades, the reality is that after some time, a tension will arise that cannot be ignored. That's because of the opposite truth that has also lived within us since our first year of existence:

We are all curious beings with a strong sense of agency.

Regardless of the mother's feelings about the short sofa drop, that won't stop the baby from being curious about it. This means that one day he will tackle it, irrespective of what his mother feels about the matter. Whenever we are curious about something, our agency will call out to act upon it. This is the natural state of any child, who tries to bend any rule that prevents him from playing with what's fascinating. Such is the natural state for you and me as well.

What conditioning does, however, is to convince us that our curiosities are sources of fear. It will make us believe that our intuition is faulty, and that success or serenity will be elusive if we follow it. It will make us believe that everyone else has the answers, and that listening to our own voice is a distraction from pursuing what's practical and realistic.

This is the situation I found myself in at the depths of my depression. I had everything that I thought I was supposed to have, but none of it felt like it originated from within. Everything seemed to be a manifestation of the voices and norms that shaped my pursuits, starting from my upbringing and culminating in adulthood. This led to the feeling that I didn't know who I was, and that my life was sculpted by a series of hands, none of which were my own.

When you are suffering, you do so because you don't understand who you truly are. Every thread of mental anguish ties back to an inability to trust yourself, which makes you outsource your thoughts and actions to an outside entity. But given that contentment can only be found within, the tendency to deny your intuition is the surest route to discontent.

Remember: Conditioning is the source of all

suffering. Once you internalize this, things will never be the same.

CHAPTER 3
A BRIEF DETOUR OF PHYSICAL DISTRESS

BEFORE WE PROCEED ONWARD, I want to address an objection you may have. Based on what we went over in the last chapter, you might be thinking:

"Wait, conditioning is the source of *all* suffering? What if I had a physical condition that's causing me great pain? How does that connect to an inability to trust myself?"

This is a great question, and I want to start by discussing a health issue of my own.

In December 2019, I was sitting in my room when for no apparent reason, a high-frequency sound emerged in my right ear. You can think of it as a buzz or hum that emanates from power lines, only pitched a few octaves higher. I first thought there was a loose wire in my room that was causing the noise, but I couldn't find anything of the sort. It was deeply unpleasant, and it disturbed my mental state for the day.

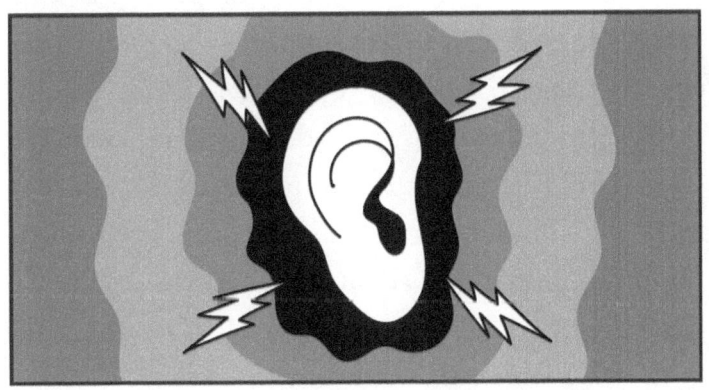

I managed to fall asleep with this high-pitch sound in my ear, only to be greeted by it the next morning. To my horror, it wouldn't go away. It persisted and kept buzzing along, regardless of how much I wanted it to fade. Sleepless nights and stressful days followed as I tried desperately to look for something that would resolve this condition (known as tinnitus). I tried medication, herbs, homeopathy, and acupuncture in an attempt to eliminate it. Weeks passed, and nothing worked.

I was very troubled, and in this state, I wanted to ease my nerves by talking about it with some friends. When I discussed my struggles, most of them didn't even know what tinnitus was, but to my surprise, one of them revealed that he had it himself. In fact, he'd had it for well over a decade and it continued to persist.

When he told me this, my heart dropped. *Was that going to be me as well? Is this something that's just a part of my life now? What was I going to do?*

As these questions swirled around my mind, I asked him what measures he took to help ease the ringing and humming. And to that, he simply replied, "I don't do anything about it. It's just there, and I don't expect it to go away."

I don't expect it to go away.

When I heard that sentence, I had a realization: My tinnitus started long ago, but my expectations of what *should* happen was the source of my misery. The buzzing in my ear was my pain, but my desire for its dissipation was my suffering.

Physical health is one of those domains where pain is inescapable. Entropy ensures that cells rupture, organs fail, and in my case, neurons misfire. This all escalates until one day, life itself falls to the hands of disorder and ceases to exist.

But the beautiful balance is that our minds have the astounding ability to reframe our bodily sensations. In extreme cases, you have someone like Quảng Đức, a Vietnamese monk who famously engulfed himself in flames as he sat in total silence. There is no doubt that he was in incredible pain on the day of his death, yet his demeanor exuded a sense of peace. Of course, neither you nor I want to replicate this dynamic, but it shows you what the mind is capable of.

The more fitting lesson for us is that suffering is a mental interpretation of our physical reality. The reason why chronic conditions cause great suffering is because the desire for its elimination is equally great. All you want is to be restored to a prior version of yourself, who was healthier and happier than the person you are now.

And it is here where we arrive at the answer to this chapter's opening question.

Anytime you have an expectation of becoming something you are not, that is conditioning. This

doesn't only apply to other people, but also to prior versions of yourself. This may sound strange, but the truth often is.

What's implicit in the desire for a past restoration is the belief that you—as you are now—are incapable of feeling the contentment you once had. This belief tends to be most salient when you're under physical distress because you're so aware of everything that has changed. But the truth is, you're chasing something that is not you anymore, and any external pursuit of this nature is conditioning.

Of course, this doesn't mean that if a promising procedure (or source of relief) emerges, you should deny it. That's not the point I'm making here. What I mean is that if you're expecting a specific outcome of that procedure, then you are making yourself vulnerable to suffering. Anytime you have an expectation to be restored to a prior state, you will be fixated on that version of yourself, and any attachment of this kind will disturb you.

It's been many years since my tinnitus first emerged, and it hasn't gone away as of this date. But the difference is that now, I don't expect it to. Sure, if a promising cure comes up, I may look into it, but I have no expectations that it'll restore me to what I once was. This is because I now understand that **contentment**

doesn't reside in what you previously were, but rather in an embrace of what you currently are. That trust in who I am now is how I've come to peace with my condition.

Despite knowing that death is inevitable, we are somehow convinced that our bodies will remain healthy until that day. This is also a product of subtle conditioning, whether it's in the form of lofty promises or distorted beliefs that are dispensed by others. The truth, of course, is that all of nature follows a decay function, and none of us are immune. So the thing to consider is if you can accept the pain that accompanies the human body, while also reducing the suffering using the power of the human mind.

CHAPTER 4
WHY WE ACCEPT OUR CONDITIONING

NOW THAT WE'VE addressed the point of physical pain, we can continue onward on our path to self-understanding. And speaking of paths, this is a good time to introduce an analogy that will help us understand our relationship to conditioning.

Imagine that you're hiking and you come across a fork in the trail. On one side, you see a path that is well-traveled and void of any obstructions. There are countless footprints that have been inked into the damp path, indicating a strong track record of reliability. You can clearly see where the path ends, revealing the scenic destination that your trek would culminate in.

The other path, however, asks more of your imagination. It's not completely obstructed, but there are many patches of thick foliage and boulders that you'll have to wade through. You don't see any footprints in the mud, but you get the vague sense that people have been here before. Unlike the other route, there's no clear vantage point you can see at the end, but you get the feeling that it does culminate somewhere.

Now, the obvious question would be to ask which path you'd take, but here's a more interesting framing:

If this were the 1st time you came to this fork, which path would you take?

What if it were the 10th time?

And what if it were the 100th time?

Feel free to sit with these inquiries for a moment before proceeding.

Okay.

Chances are, your responses to these questions would be different, and this dynamic reveals the mechanics of conditioning.

Anytime we are in an unfamiliar environment, there are two opposing forces that emerge:

1. The push for certainty, and
2. The pull toward curiosity.

The push for certainty is driven by **fear**, whereas the pull toward curiosity is driven by **play**. At first, certainty will defeat curiosity because our fear response is heightened. But over time, curiosity will reign as we strive to be tested and challenged.

Let's see how this insight plays out in our thought experiment.

When you see the fork for the first time, the well-paved path will scream for your attention because the whole situation is foreign. The mind will seek the option that seems most reliable, which is signaled through the affirmations of others. If a lot of people have chosen a given path, then it must be safe, and this feeling of safety alleviates our fear of the unknown. So given this dynamic, this is the path we'll likely take.

But at the same time, a seed will also have been planted by the pull of curiosity.

The imagination is helplessly drawn to wonder, and its object of fixation will be that of the other path.

Where does that one lead? How difficult or easy will it be? What are some of the obstacles that may be there?

These are the questions that will arise as you leave it behind for the time being.

If this were the 10th time you've visited this fork, the action you take may be the same but the thoughts you have will differ. While certainty may still edge out over curiosity, its draw won't be as powerful as it once was. You might still take the well-traveled path, but the desire to satiate your imagination will grow stronger. Instead of wondering where the questionable path leads, you'll tell yourself that one day, you'll see for yourself. This is because our sense of agency grows as our fear of the unknown fades, and this is where curiosity begins to take the helm.

By the 100th time, it's highly likely that you've already checked out the other path, and have emerged from it knowing that everything was all right. (If anything, you'll give yourself a hard time for not having embarked on it earlier.) However, if you haven't stepped onto the other path yet, the questions you have won't be directed to the route, but **rather to yourself**.

Why can't you get yourself to venture onto it? What are you so scared of? How much longer will you suppress your sense of wonderment?

Choosing certainty is only desirable when we fear the unknown. But as that fear fades, choosing curiosity is the next logical step. And when you don't take that step, it'll feel like you're limiting the scope of meaningful experiences you can have. This is a version of suffering that countless people feel, all because of an ardent attachment to safety.

And it is this very attachment that makes us accept our conditioning.

At its core, **fear is the tension of uncertainty**. Almost any fear you can think of—whether it relates to health, wealth, or relationships—is tied to the desire for an anticipated result. People that are sick, for example, fear that they won't get better. People worrying about money fear that they'll never have enough. It's not the thing itself that breeds fear, but the uncertainty that accompanies it.

Conditioning is alluring because it promises

certainty in what to expect. Whether it is presented as a pathway to prestige, a rulebook to socialization, or a roadmap to status, it's an external force that helps you regulate your inner insecurities. It assures you that certainty is attainable if you look to what's already been done, and this is comforting in a world that evades prediction.

But as our hiking analogy showed, there comes a point where the fear of uncertainty transitions to an acceptance of it. We begin to question our conditioning and the allure of a well-traveled path, even if it feels safe to follow it.

That's because we can no longer deny the voice within us that upholds curiosity and agency above all else. This is the result of an intricate blend of life experiences, interests, and perspectives that only you can have, which all coalesce to form what we call your **intuition**. This is the greatest asset we've been gifted, but sadly, we tend to defer its influence to other voices instead.

So in the next chapter, we're going to explore the power of this inner gift. And in doing so, we'll set the foundation for a brighter path forward; one that allows us to trust our ability to solve the greatest challenges we face.

CHAPTER 5
INTUITION AND THE INNER COMPASS

Let's start by defining what intuition is.

Some say that it's a gut feeling that validates a decision. Others think of it as an alarm that alerts you of potential mishaps. And in some circles, it might be described as a divine force that guides you toward truth.

Regardless of which framing you use, there is utility in each one. That's because we all recognize that the world is unpredictable, yet we still have to navigate it with confidence. If you want to make the most of life, you have to lean into it instead of shrinking from it, and that is only made possible through a belief that you can handle the unknown.

Intuition is the inner wisdom that welcomes uncertainty. It understands that you can't know everything, but what you know about yourself will make up for that gap. And by trusting your resolve, you're able to frame the unknown in a way that serves you.

To illustrate this dynamic, let's consider the three main factors that will have an outsized impact on your life:

1. Where you live,
2. What you work on, and
3. Who you're with.

You can get many things wrong, but if you get the above three right, your well-being will be high. So for something this important, you might assume that rationality will be the beacon that guides you toward the answer. Perhaps you'll do a ton of research, make a list of various factors, and make your decisions based on a careful weighing of your options.

What you'll find, however, is that a pros and cons list can only take you so far. What looks good on paper may feel off in spirit, and the inverse is also true. For example, a job offer that checks all the boxes can still feel like it's the wrong one. Or a date that doesn't satisfy your initial criteria can later feel like the right partner. There is a limit as to how far your rationality can take you, and it's not as far as you might think.

Intuition is what takes you from the limits of logic to the decision you ultimately make. No matter how rigorously you apply reason to reduce uncertainty, there will always be a great level of uncertainty you have to accept. Your intuition is what helps you make that jump, knowing that this specific texture of the unknown is a worthwhile challenge to navigate. You can't predict what a big move or a career change will yield, but your intuition instills the confidence required to welcome whatever does.

One way to imagine intuition at work is in the form of an inner compass we all have:

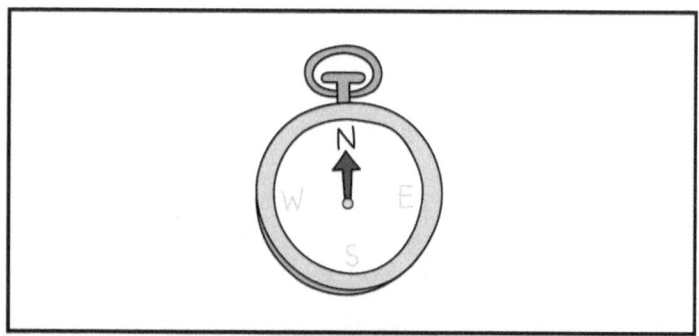

Every inner compass starts at true north, which is the state of trusting ourselves. This is because we are all born with the gift of presence (as discussed in Chapter

2), which is when your inner state is in alignment with your external surroundings. There's no worry or fear when you're present because you're content with what simply is. This is why children are fully attentive to whatever is in front of them, and why adults feel time dissolve when we're in a state of flow. We are all capable of feeling this because this very state is the origin of our minds.

When your compass is at true north, you have **conviction** in who you are. You're aware that uncertainty is inevitable, but it's a source of empowerment rather than fear. The fact that you can't predict what happens next is seen as a feature of life, and not a bug. After all, if everything was knowable, there would be no room for curiosity to emerge. Curiosity is being grateful that there's more to uncover, which is what drives the conviction to explore.

Now, if our inner compasses stayed here, we would all be doing what is aligned with our sense of purpose. But as we all know, there are many forces that prevent us from doing just that.

What disturbs this alignment are the winds of **conditioning**. This is when the external voices promising security, safety, and status direct us to a path that is not our own, which ultimately leads to suffering. Conditioning takes many forms, but in the context of the inner compass, any force that pulls you away from true north falls under its reach.

CONDITIONING

Anytime you think you "should" do something, that's conditioning. Anytime you compare yourself to another, that's conditioning. Anything that causes fear or worry to arise is conditioning, as peace is disturbed only when you have an expectation that lies beyond the present moment.

The great thing about your inner compass, however, is that it does a great job alerting you of when these winds are pulling you away from true north. And the way it does that is through the avenue of your physiology.

This may sound a bit esoteric, so I'll take a moment to explain.

Let's say that you're working at a job you find meaningful. You're solving problems you care about with people you care for, and this creates an atmosphere of purpose. The only gripe is that the pay could be higher, but you recognize that it's enough for your needs.

Now let's say that a recruiter approaches you for another job, which will effectively double your pay. The tradeoff, however, is that you'll have to take up more managerial responsibilities, which don't align with your inherent interests. What you give up in agency will be made whole through money, and that is the state of the offer.

Upon learning about this opportunity, you'll likely feel a tension arise somewhere in your body. Some common areas are the chest, stomach, or forehead, but it's a familiar area where tensions of this kind arise. You may initially interpret it as anxiety or stress, but what's really happening is that your inner compass is alerting you of a pull away from true north (in some cases, it feels like a literal pull on your body). It's telling you that the winds of conditioning are strong, and that there's a chance you may go against your intuition as a result.

If you were already doing meaningful work and making enough money, then your inner compass is asking you why you'd want the other opportunity. More money is great, but is it worth a misalignment in your interests? If you're feeling challenged in all the right ways, why are you trading that away for a certainty you don't care much for? At the center of all this is the allure for something external, which manifests in the form of expectations of what you "should" do.

It was once believed that mind and body were separate entities (an idea known as dualism), but both neuroscience and philosophy have converged to show that they are closely interlinked. The inner compass is one way of illustrating just how connected these two realms are, and in this case, how a conflict within the mind manifests as a pressure in the body. This reveals a fundamental truth about how the inner landscape works:

When you are conditioned, every action feels tense. But when you have conviction, every action feels fluid.

The Daoists have a concept called wu-wei, which roughly translates to "effortless action." It recognizes that we have to act within this world, but that we can do so in a way that harmonizes with its natural order. Instead of controlling our way through existence, we can locate its seams and ride alongside them.

This is what having conviction feels like. When you trust your intuition, you recognize your innate capabilities and see all the ways in which they fit within the world. There is an alignment between who you are and what you offer, so you develop the confidence to lean into what makes you unique.

Conditioning, on the other hand, is filled with tension because you're constantly trying to insert your-self into unwelcoming terrain. Instead of leaning into your innate curiosities, you shrink away from them and mold yourself according to the preferences of others. And in doing so, you open the floodgates of suffering because this terrain is where fear, envy, and competition reside.

Ultimately, every endeavor comes down to two options. **You can either choose conviction, or choose conditioning.** You can follow your true north, or be swayed by external winds. You can choose what you must do, or what you should do.

This is what the inner compass helps you calibrate throughout your days.

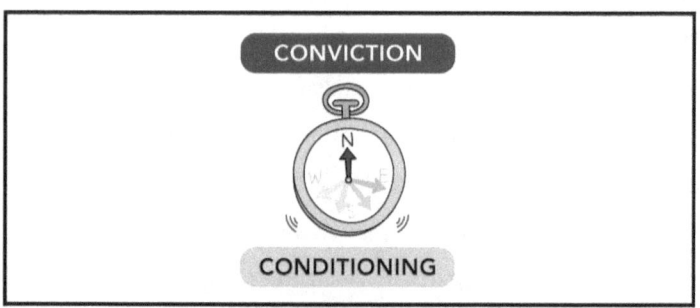

When you see life as a choice between conviction and conditioning, there is a clarity that accompanies that lens. You see how every pursuit has two clear endpoints depending on which path you choose.

To illustrate this, here's how the inner compass is delineated in four meaningful domains:

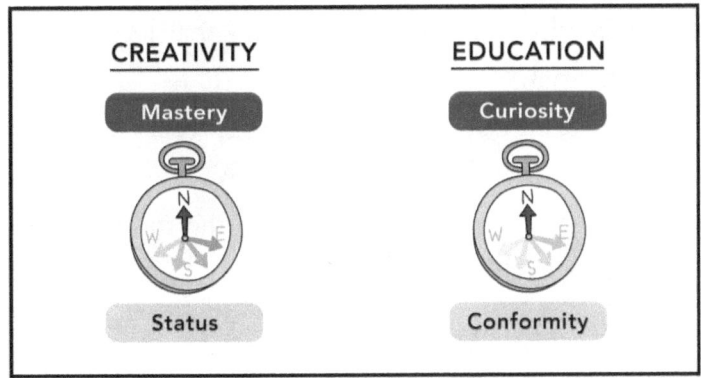

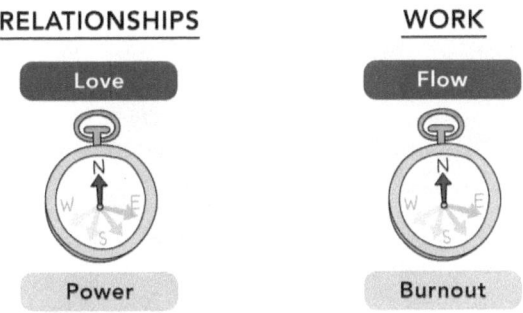

We will go into some of these domains later in the book, but you can immediately see the difference between trusting your intuition and denying it. True north points to the heights of what we have to offer, while conditioning caters to the lowest of our impulses.

With that said, a common objection to the above is the following:

"Wait, but what if your intuition is faulty? If you

trust something that is flawed, won't that just lead to bad outcomes?"

It's a good question, and one that we'll go over in the next chapter. And in doing so, we'll explore why the pursuit of self-understanding is the most worthwhile of them all.

CHAPTER 6
THE MAGNETISM OF
KNOWING YOURSELF

WHENEVER YOU DISCUSS the power of following your intuition, you'll get one of two responses:

1. A wholehearted agreement, or
2. A skeptical dismissal.

What's interesting is that both responses have merit. There are times when intuition needs to be embraced, and times when it needs to be questioned.

For example, when you're a toddler, it's safe to say that your intuition isn't the best thing to follow. At that age, all that matters is the potential for a situation to be fun, which can involve all sorts of physical dangers. You might feel compelled to tumble down a set of stairs because it seems exciting, but the ensuing pain will give your intuition a much-needed update. While this seems like a rather elementary example, the truth is that this same dynamic applies to our adult lives as well.

Perhaps there was a time in your life where you were so certain about the kind of work you wanted to do, only to realize that it was a terrible fit. Or your intuition pointed you to "a dream partner," only to reveal that this was the last person you needed in your life. There may have been many moments, big or small, that carried this texture of surprise.

While this may make you question the accuracy of your intuition, what's undeniable is that these missteps yielded insights. And paradoxically, these very insights are what shape your intuition and make it so valuable over time.

Intuition needs to be stress tested by reality to earn its reliability. It has to first show you how it was wrong so that you can trust that it's learned all the lessons required for it to be right. This constant dance between setback and growth is what fuels confidence in your own judgments, which is what gives rise to your resolve.

Age and wisdom tend to be directly correlated because age yields experience, and experience yields lessons. But what if there was a way to gain this wisdom without all the wrinkles and conflict that accompany it? How can you align your intuition without having to rely upon decades of testing it with the outside world to do so?

The answer resides in one simple word: **self-understanding**. Because the more you know yourself, the less you look to others to show you what the world is like. By being aware of both your capabilities and limitations, you'll know exactly how to navigate the world in a way that feels fluid and aligned with your values. The best part is that the pursuit of self-understanding can start at any age, regardless of who you are. Intention is the only requisite to begin.

In the context of the inner compass, I view self-understanding as the magnet that keeps you aligned to true north:

It is only through knowing yourself where you can trust that your intuition is guiding you to the right place. Without self-understanding, you will always use external validation as a proxy for what you want and how you'll get it. This leads to an outsourcing of your intuition to other minds, which means that you'll never learn how to trust your own judgment.

We tend to embody this mindset when we're young because self-understanding is discouraged by almost everyone. Teachers want you to follow their curriculums, parents want you to follow their rules, and peers want you to follow their preferences. Conformity takes precedence over curiosity, and this is what makes a young mind so impressionable. At this age, the magnet of self-understanding is tiny and weak, which is why the winds of conditioning easily blow the hands of your compass away.

This explains why students desire career paths that everyone else is chasing. Or why physical attractiveness is the only item on everyone's checklist. Or why anyone that seems unfamiliar is a candidate for bullying. You are conditioned to pursue what is deemed valuable by the masses, and this dynamic caters to the lowest of our impulses.

You may assume that the above applies primarily to the young, but sadly, it is just as prevalent in the old. Many adults have the temperament of toddlers because they've never made an effort to know themselves. In an unexamined mind, the relentless pursuit of status comes at the expense of compassion, and the worst part is that it's not even aware of this transaction. But as we all know, misery catches up to the person who treats humanity as a means to their ends.

Those of us that see the power of self-understanding envision a brighter path, and want to lean into our intuition to lift us out of our conditioning. We begin to question what we want, knowing that those wants weren't planted by our own hands. We start to design our own intellectual pursuits, knowing that curiosity is the glue that holds them together. Bit by bit, we build up our magnet, which brings the pointer of the compass closer to true north.

In the initial stages, we are still susceptible to the winds of conditioning because self-understanding is nowhere near as easy as it sounds. Socrates famously distilled all of contemplative thought into the imperative to "know yourself," realizing that those two words were the answer to life's greatest questions. Embedded in every meaningful pursuit is difficulty, and given that this pursuit is the most meaningful of them all, there will be many hurdles to face.

But here's the thing. What's difficult can still be simple, and the truth is that self-understanding retains this simplicity. I've realized that for something as grandiose as self-understanding, it can be cultivated through the consistent application of just three principles. Each principle is a single word, and it is through these three words that your magnet will be constructed and maintained. Like anything worthwhile, this takes dedication to put into practice, but once you do, you'll see how your intuition is fully aligned with your being.

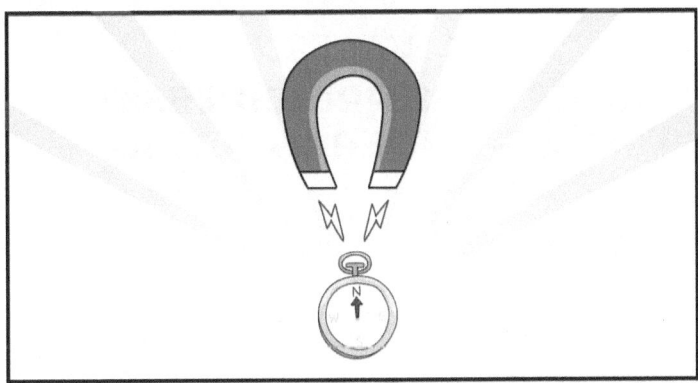

Socrates provided the imperative, but didn't detail the approach. The remainder of this book is my attempt to outline an approach in the form of three principles that anyone can internalize, regardless of age or background. Applying them changed the course of my life, from lifting me out of depression to imbuing a sense of purpose in my days. Knowing yourself is the antidote to suffering, and the mere awareness of this truth is half the journey.

The remaining half is what you do after having that realization, which is where the next chapter begins.

CHAPTER 7
THE THREE PRINCIPLES OF SELF-UNDERSTANDING

PARADOXICALLY, knowing yourself doesn't happen in isolation.

While being alone with your mind is a feature of the process, it is just that: a feature. The process itself extends well beyond it, encompassing all the interactions you have with other people as well. This is because no being can exist without the other, as the social nature of our species ensures that to be the case.

Life is a single-player game, but meaning is derived on multi-player mode. You're responsible for the actions you take, but the results of those actions will be shared amongst others. Everything you do contributes to the state of the world, irrespective of how large or small you think that impact may be.

A simple way to map this dynamic is in the form of this diagram:

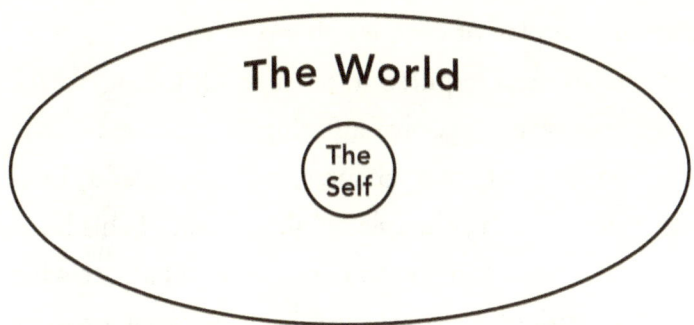

There is you, the self, that is a part of the greater world you inhabit. And much of self-understanding is about knowing how to function within this world while retaining conviction in who you are. Attaining this balance is the hallmark of what it means to know yourself.

It is with this context that I'd now like to share the three principles of self-understanding. They are:

1. Reflect
2. Relate
3. Create

That's it. Three simple words that house an abundance of detail.

Each principle touches upon a section of the "Self and the World" map shown earlier, as every component is necessary to comprehend. It is through the careful interplay of each moving part where you cultivate the stillness required to resist conditioning, which is the only way to dissolve suffering.

The rest of this chapter will provide a brief summary of each principle, while the rest of this book will explore them in greater depth. The details are what produce insight, but the overviews are what provoke curiosity. So with that aim in mind, let's briefly review what each principle entails.

REFLECT.

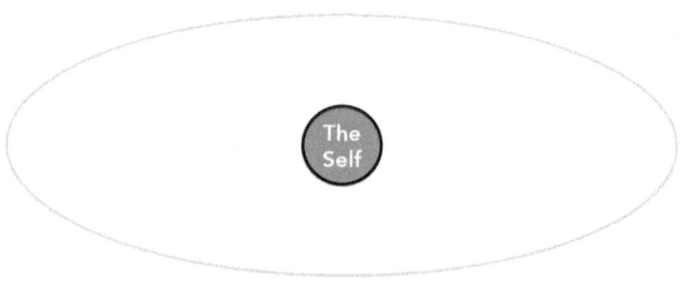

The foundation of your being has been built by other hands. Your genes, your parents, and your upbringing are the result of randomness, yet they are responsible for much of your worldview.

The first principle of reflection starts with the recognition of this fact, then attempts to take a bottom-up approach to the question of who you are. It's an active exploration of the building blocks of your identity, an understanding of why they're there, and the discernment of what to keep or replace. What results is the core of who you are, untouched by the winds of conditioning and free from the fog of fear.

To reflect is to study the self and to question what you find. And through this process, you'll develop the conviction required to position yourself within the world.

RELATE.

Relationship is a mirror. The way you view others will reflect the way you view yourself.

If you treat people as assets that serve your goals, then you will define yourself by what you produce. If you categorize people by status, then you'll use your place in society to determine your self-worth.

Conversely, if you treat people with compassion, then you will be kind to yourself regardless of circumstance. If you are present with whoever you encounter, then you'll retain contentment even when you're alone.

To relate is to study the world and how you interact with it. And through this process, you'll discover an unfiltered perception of who you are.

CREATE.

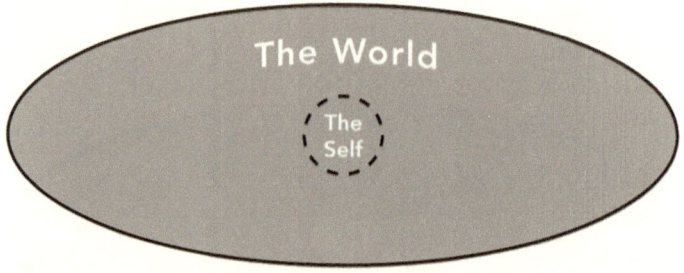

Creating is not a privilege reserved for the artistic few. It's a birthright that we all have access to, and exercising it dissolves the boundary between you and the other.

Take a brief moment to look at your surroundings.

Almost everything you see, from this book you're holding to the contents of your environment, is the result of creativity. Creating and sharing is in the lifeblood of our species, and it is through this dynamic where we construct our reality and coexist within it.

To create is to express what you've discovered about yourself and the world. And through this process, you'll harvest meaning from the experiences that have deep roots in your mind.

———

Reflect. Relate. Create.

In the pages that follow, we'll explore each principle in sequential order, largely because each one feeds off its precedent. **Reflection** is the origin point because it's only through questioning yourself where you observe your unconditioned core. By observing this core, you then gain clarity into the kinds of **relationships** that will brighten both yours and others. And by knowing what brightens yourself and others, you then **create** the very things that contribute to that shared brilliance.

Through this cycle, you strengthen your sense of purpose and gain a better understanding of who you are. And given that the journey of self-understanding has no endpoint, each step forward is yet another opportunity for reflection, which brings us back to where it all begins.

CHAPTER 8
REFLECT: THE ART OF QUESTIONING YOUR MIND

66 For him who has conquered the mind, the mind is the best of friends; but for one who has failed to do so, his mind will remain the greatest enemy.

BHAGAVAD GITA

WISDOM IS the co-existence of contradictory truths. It's to understand that every truth contains the seed of its opposite, and nowhere is this more pertinent than in the domain of the mind.

What gives the mind an incredible capacity for self-awareness also lends itself to self-deception. I'm reminded of this whenever I sit down to meditate, only to be bombarded by thoughts of things I need to do or demands I have to fulfill. The very mind that encourages me to sit in stillness also produces the disturbances that nullifies this objective. Its ability to dispense false (yet believable) narratives is unparalleled, and it can do so even when I'm most aware of when it's happening.

This is because the mind has been shaped by decades of conditioning, all of which give rise to an incessant chatter about how you must satisfy external expectations. Take the feeling of worry, for example. Worry is the belief that you're not satisfying a specific expectation, *even after you've done your best to satisfy it.* Rather than leave it up to forces outside your control, your attachment to an outcome will make you believe that worrying gives you the control you desperately desire. This just leads to sleepless nights and pointless suffering, but it's astounding what a conditioned mind can make you justify.

Reflection breaks the pattern of being helplessly shepherded by your thoughts. Given that an unchecked mind bends toward rumination, reflection is the checking mechanism that redirects it toward insight. The question, of course, is how exactly one does this.

Earlier I mentioned meditation, but I want to start by stating that meditation is *not* reflection. This may sound odd, given that meditation is one of the more popular practices people use to still the mind. But that's because we need to define what we mean by "reflection," and how meditation doesn't fit that criteria.

The key difference is this: **Reflection is an active phenomenon, whereas meditation is not.** Reflection is about asking questions, recognizing patterns, and studying your mind to calibrate your inner compass. Meditation, on the other hand, is the art of doing nothing. It's to remove the pull of questions and to dissolve the sense of self so your mind can finally be quiet.

If you're meditating, then by definition, you're not reflecting. Meditation is the *absence* of thought to achieve stillness, whereas reflection is the *usage* of thought to achieve clarity. They are two wholly different things that are often mistaken for one another.

We are going to focus on reflection because it's only through an active exploration of the self where you can identify your conditioning. The more diligent you are about questioning what you feel, the closer you get to the assumptions that are driving those emotions. And by removing the assumptions that were planted by others, the clearer you become about who you are.

With that said, where do we begin?

Well, if the objective is to reduce suffering, then an ideal target for reflection is anything that provokes tension. Recall that the inner compass alerts you of any miscalibrations through your physiology, whether it's in the form of a tight chest, knotted stomach, or any other place in the body where this usually materializes. Whenever this happens, there is a mantra of sorts I keep in mind, which is this:

Wherever there's tension, there's a tale.

If you dig into anything that causes fear, at the root is some tale that's been planted by another. Chances are, this story was embedded when you were at your most impressionable, and many of your unconscious behaviors are outgrowths of it. By identifying what it is, you're then capable of reframing it as a fairy tale that holds no place in reality.

For example, a common source of fear we have is money. This is one of those domains where the imagination runs wild, which then conjures anxiety about the future. And because money is always a narrative issue, this fear is pervasive across all economic classes, from billionaires to the impoverished to everyone in between.

So here we've identified an object of tension, which is money. But what's causing the tension isn't money (which is value-neutral), but rather the story that's been inherited about it. So the next step in the process of reflection is to pinpoint what that story is, and that is accomplished through a simple yet profound inquiry:

This ability to ask "why" is what differentiates humanity from any other species on the planet. A gorilla and caveman may have navigated the material world in similar ways, but only the human looked up at the sky and wondered why we were here. This led to the birth of myths, religions, philosophy, and every other story attempting to explain our relationship to the world at large.

Similarly, the ability to ask "Why?" in the context of your own life can lead to dramatic outcomes. By directing this question toward your sources of tension, you can dig in and locate the conditioned seed that resides at the heart of it. And by replacing that seed with your own conviction, you're able to convert that tension into a source of empowerment.

I mentioned money earlier because it acts as a personal case study of sorts. My money fears manifested in a rather interesting way, which was through an intense fear of being homeless. Rather than viewing money as a generator of wealth, I viewed it as a safety net that kept me from sleeping on the streets. This was a fear that afflicted me for many years, which led to a distorted perception of money's role in my life.

As I began to understand the power of reflection, it was obvious that this was a tension I needed to address. And it all started with an effortful questioning of why that fear was so salient.

Now, there are many techniques that offer to help you with this process (like asking "Why?" five times in succession, etc.), but this book isn't about tactics. It's about the principles, which are timeless and are meant to be adapted to your own preferences. What matters is that you're determined to get to the core narrative driving that tension, and to then **reframe it**. That latter part is perhaps the most important step of them all.

In my case, I grew to understand that the core of my money fears came from my upbringing. For example, I have a clear memory of my parents telling me that you can dig in the dirt all you want, but you'll never find a dollar. The narrative was that money is an incredibly scarce resource that you have to work hard for, and crucially, on the right things. While the sentiment makes sense, the problem is that I framed the "incredibly scarce" part of the lesson and made that my entire story.

This is why it's not enough to simply identify the source of tension. If that were the case, I'd be tempted to blame my parents for my fears and leave it at that. The reality is that they were just trying to teach me the value of a dollar, but I didn't have the self-awareness to extract the wisdom of that lesson when I was young. Instead, I took in the worst of it and it became my conditioning.

This is precisely what reflection helps you correct. It helps you realize that you have the agency to contextualize what you've heard, and that you can shift it a few degrees closer to the truth.

So once I understood the source of my money fears, I made a conscious attempt to reframe it. I asked myself why I thought money was so scarce, which led me to the answer that my family didn't have much of it. That was an objective fact.

But here's the interesting thing.

Despite growing up poor, I didn't *feel* poor. Since I grew up in a loving community and my parents were so present, I always felt like there was an abundance of warmth and safety throughout my days. There was a disconnect between *being* poor and *feeling* poor, and what made that possible was the love that permeated our household.

This realization changed everything. What I understood then was that homelessness wasn't about the poverty of money, but the poverty of love. Even if I lost all my money, I wouldn't go homeless because there were too many people that cared for me. Any one of these individuals would ensure that I had somewhere to stay while I figured out whatever came next. I viscerally understood that the abundance of compassion would overcome any scarcity of currency.

Once I reached this point of understanding, my fear of homelessness dissipated, and has remained silent ever since. What took its place was a deep conviction that everything would be okay, and that money was a tool that allowed me to spend my attention in fruitful ways. It became a resource of freedom rather than a symbol of fear, and that perspective shift did wonders for my relationship with money.

The beautiful thing is that this process of reflection is applicable to any domain in life. I highlighted money here because it's an area you can likely relate to, but just remember that wherever there's tension, there's a tale. Any source of tension can be alleviated by (1) identifying the tale that's been planted, and by (2) reframing it to serve you.

In other words, you strip away your conditioning, and replace it with your conviction. This is an iterative process, but just know that your intuition will strengthen with each subsequent turn.

With that said, you might be wondering:

"Wait, do I just do all this reflection stuff in my head and expect to arrive at an answer? That sounds like a recipe for overthinking, which can make things worse. How do I reflect in a way that doesn't feel like I'm trapped inside of my own mind?"

This is a great question, and one that's important to address. Since the mind can produce the very problems you're looking to solve, you don't want to rely purely on the intellect to guide you.

So in the next chapter, I'll introduce a practice that will help you navigate your mind without getting tangled up in it. It's a practice that will release your thoughts instead of holding them in, which provides the clarity required to reframe any fears you may have.

CHAPTER 9
WRITE FOR YOURSELF, AND WISDOM WILL FOLLOW

We write everyday; it just doesn't feel that way.

Sending a text message doesn't feel like writing, but it is. Using a search engine doesn't feel like writing, but it is. Drafting a to-do list doesn't feel like writing, but it is.

We often think of writing as a lofty art form that's reserved for authors, but it's something we all do everyday. Anytime you deliver a thought in a readable format, that's writing. The issue, however, is that this act has been so integrated into our daily lives that we rarely recognize its power. One of the hallmarks of a successful technology is that we no longer notice it as such, and in that regard, writing is perhaps the most successful of them all.

So here's a question I'd like to propose: **If writing**

has been so effective at helping us navigate the world, how effective would it be in helping us navigate ourselves? If we recognized the power of writing and directed it toward the inner compass instead, what type of insights might arise as a result?

Given that we all write everyday, the goal here isn't to invent anything new. Rather, it's to expand your usage of writing beyond the functional realm and into the reflective one. Instead of using the written word to get things done, also use it to explore your mind and identify where it's been conditioned. If you approach writing with this type of intention, then it can be transformed into an indispensable practice that aids in the process of self-understanding.

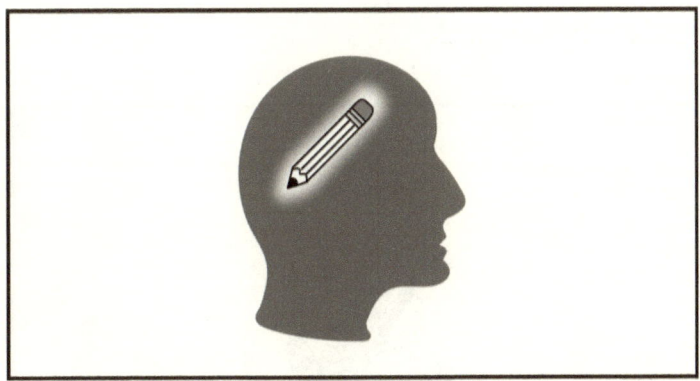

Now, you might be asking why writing is the best medium for this objective. After all, you can go out for a leisurely walk to sort through your thoughts, create some voice recordings, or do any number of things that help you reflect on the trajectory of your life. So why write?

The reason is simple. When you write, you cannot do anything else but put words on a page, and it's this very act of sitting with your mind that makes the practice so powerful. With each word you write, you are converting a present thought into a readable artifact that brings a sense of order to how you think. Even if the words don't make sense in the moment, the fact that you're writing them down signals your commitment to understanding them in the future. Writing turns you into a historian of your life, which helps you identify the old stories you've inherited so that they can later be reframed.

Knowing this, the objective of writing here is to learn about who you are and how you operate. That's it. It's not to express yourself or to share your ideas with others (this is a topic for another principle). You are writing purely for yourself, so what matters isn't whether the writing is any good, but that you showed up to write in the first place. Presence precedes prose in the domain of reflection.

So the next question, of course, is what exactly you write about. If you're writing whatever comes to mind each day, won't this just become a diary of sorts? What's the use in that?

This is a good time to make a distinction between a diary and a journal. A diary is when you write about the "what"s of life: what you did, what you want, and what you felt. For example, the beginning of a diary entry might look like this:

> Today I went to a work party and felt anxious the whole time. I felt like I didn't belong there but tried to fit in anyway. I don't like how I try to fit in even when I feel misaligned with the group, as it feels like a form of self-deception. I'll keep this in mind the next time I'm in this situation.

A journal, on the other hand, is about the "why"s of life: *why* you did it, *why* you wanted it, and *why* you felt it. And given that reflection is all about asking the "why" behind everything, a journal is the very thing we want to be keeping.

For example, this may be the journal version of the prior entry:

> *Today I went to a work party and felt anxious because my colleagues don't share the same values as me. My core value is about following my curiosity, but theirs is about maximizing earnings. I tried to fit in anyway because I need to appear interested to keep my job, but at the same time, do I really need this job anymore? Why am I still keeping this job when I have a decent amount of money saved up?*

Notice how the journal entry invites deeper exploration through words like "because" and "why" in a way that the diary entry doesn't. It recognizes patterns, identifies behaviors, and most importantly, questions assumptions. Reflection is about sifting through the noise to get to the core of why a feeling exists, which helps you see the conditioning at the bottom of it all.

You could imagine that if I took the final question to its conclusion, I'll find some expectation or norm that's driving the anxiety that was felt at the work party. It is only then where I can begin reframing it to produce a healthier behavior going forward.

One thing I want to clarify is that your journal doesn't have to make sense, nor does it have to sound coherent. The above entry was written rather lucidly to act as a comprehensible example, but most journal entries will sound like gibberish. *And that's the point.*

When you're reflecting, you don't want your thoughts to be trapped in your head. Rather, you want to quickly let them out so it feels like you've released them somewhere, as it's only through that release where you don't feel so attached to them. This requires you to remove the dam of doubt and let the torrent of thoughts flow onto the page. In doing so, you become an observer of your thoughts, which gives you the distance required to perceive them without bias.

When you use feeling as the guide (rather than the intellect), what you lose in order is gained through catharsis. Your thoughts will be jumbled and messy, but they will shine with vulnerability and honesty. This is precisely what you want, given that no one will be reading them but you. Reflection works best when your thoughts are unfiltered, as that's when you're closest to the core of who you really are.

A good place to start would be to fill a whole page each day with whatever comes to mind. In my case, I started on a mini-notebook that only fit a few sentences per page, and gradually worked my way up to a letter-size notebook that now holds a few paragraphs each. As noted earlier, the entries that will yield most insights are the journal ones (which focus on the "why"), but it's inevitable that some days will take the form of diary ones (which focus on the "what"). This is fine, given that the consistency in which you write is more important than the content of what is written. But the hope is that for every few diary entries, you have at least one journal entry that seeks to dive deeper into why you operate the way you do.

What you'll find over time is that when you know why a problem exists, the solution becomes obvious. When you see that a tension is the result of an expectation you've inherited, then you'll find ways to lessen the gravity of that expectation. When you realize that you put so much pressure on yourself because you want to be validated, then you'll find ways to lessen that pressure by embracing who you are now.

Embedded in every "why" is the "how" to proceed once you've had that realization. This is what writing for yourself helps you uncover, and the best part is that you don't ever need to call yourself a writer to see this. Since reflection is all about looking beyond labels (which is a form of conditioning), adopting this writing practice without identification is a beautiful vote for self-understanding.

By regularly removing labels in this way, you're able to develop the confidence required to accept your unconditioned core. That's because as you explore your mind in great detail, you'll begin to see what contentment looks like as you peel away the incentives and motives that have been layered on it from the outside. What remains is the essence of the inner world, which you can learn to accept without condition.

And it's that state—acceptance without condition —that's the greatest aspiration when it comes to our dynamic with others as well. The way we treat others is the way we treat ourselves, and this truth will determine the extent in which we're able to look in the mirror and embrace what we see.

So with that in mind, we turn to the next principle of self-understanding: the way we orient ourselves amongst the people of this world.

CHAPTER 10
RELATE: THE ABILITY TO SEE BEYOND GAMES

EVERY HUMAN BEING is connected to another, and there are no exceptions.

The monk in a cave requires assistance to alleviate her hunger. The prisoner in a cell requires supervision to ensure his safety. The influencer boasting about his independence does so on a platform that was built by others. And so on.

We are all in relationship with one another, and these very relationships allow us to survive and persist. Even if we're tempted to believe that we can function on our own accord, it will take less than a minute to realize that we are the beneficiaries of processes that have been set up on our behalf. There is a humility that arises from this epiphany, and it's this humility that helps you realize that self-understanding is also a communal affair.

The problem, however, is that we rarely interpret our connections with others as relationships. To relate to someone implies a sense of intimacy, and that word feels foreign in the context of the wider world. The reason for this is simple: Many of our connections aren't constructed by the hands of compassion and love, but rather by the claws of competition and gain.

Much of this begins in the education system, which is the breeding ground for conditioning. It is here where we're taught the fundamentals of categorization and division: that we are to be judged along a bell curve, that we are to follow a set of classroom standards, and that a few will be highlighted as emblems of success. You learn that a winner emerges at the expense of a loser, and that every win is expected to be followed up with yet another victory. And given enough time, you understand that this dynamic extends well beyond the domain of school.

In other words, you see how society is organized into a giant game. And just like any game, you understand the importance of building fruitful alliances, breaking bad ones, and applying consistent effort to forge ahead. And the more you desire to win this game, the more you'll judge others by the coldness of utility rather than the warmth of character. You will value people according to what they can do for you, as opposed to who they truly are.

This is the operating manual we've inherited, and if we never make an attempt to know ourselves, it will also become our epitaph. While playing the game may yield recognition and wealth, the reality is that those are the only two rewards the game will ever yield. And if those are the two criteria you use to judge others, then it's the only two lenses you'll ever use to judge yourself.

This is an intuitive point, but I'm alarmed at how often people miss it. If you have a relationship with someone because you expect to cash it in for future recognition, then don't be surprised at why you can't be content with who you are now. If you view people as walking business opportunities, then don't be surprised at the way you judge yourself because of the number in your bank account. **The inner critic is a reflection of the lens you use to view others.** So if you want to change the way you treat yourself, it starts with a conscious shift in the way you treat the other.

The good news is that we already know what the healthy version of a relationship is, which is personified through our closest friendships. What distinguishes a friend from an acquaintance is not the time in which the bond has lasted, but rather in **the lack of conditions** that accompanies that relationship. An acquaintance always requires conditions to stay in touch, with

78

the most prevalent examples being workplace colleagues and next-door neighbors. Once you quit your job or move to another city, you'll see just how conditional that connection was.

True friends, however, make an effort to sustain that bond regardless of what's going on. You don't do it because you have anything to gain, but rather because you simply love that person for who they are. Being in one another's company is the only thing you desire because that alone is enough.

It's no coincidence that our closest friends tend to stem from childhood and adolescence. This is because when we're young, the gamification of life hasn't fully coalesced in our minds. While we may see it in the forming of cliques and the ranking of aptitude, we are still many steps away from the arenas of work and wealth. This means that friendships created in this stage are built without the forces of social incentives that erode the purity of that bond. And because these friendships were formed outside the rules of the game, they have the chance to continue flourishing without their influence.

There is just one condition that ensures unconditional love: that there is no game to be played. There is nothing you want from the other, and there is nothing they want from you. All that matters is mutual presence, and we already know what this feels like in the context of our closest bonds. The key is to take this same dynamic and apply it to the greater world as well.

The reason this is difficult, however, is that conditioning has created an obstacle that prevents us from seeing the best in one other. While this obstacle is invisible to the eye, it is all-too-salient in the mind.

Every game is made operable through this force, and it is only through its dissolution where the game ceases to function. So in the next chapter, we will explore what this obstacle is, and how to decrease its fervor so we can view people for who they are, and not for what they have to offer.

CHAPTER 11
THE POISON OF STATUS

WHEN I WAS IN COLLEGE, I worked in an office for the first time. I wasn't used to this setting, as none of my prior jobs required me to sit in a cubicle and produce tedious reports. But while I quickly acclimated to the reality of my boxed workspace, what I couldn't get used to was something I observed amongst my colleagues:

The way their behavior changed depending on one's social standing.

If Bob held a higher title than John, then Bob would speak with a nonchalantness (and oftentimes arrogance) that he would never exhibit to his boss, Jane. And while Jane would always show up early to meetings with her boss, she would casually show up 15 minutes late to meetings with other folks. This collective charade was everywhere, and while we have a term that localizes it to the workplace ("office politics"), the truth is that this dynamic permeates many of our interactions at large.

The force that drives this charade is status, and it's our thirst for it that drives every game we play. It's what makes people feel superior to others, which makes them also assume inferiority when it comes to people they admire. Status is always zero-sum in this way; your arrogance only stretches as far as your subservience. People that act like obedient dogs in the faces of their masters will be the first to bark orders in the faces of their servants. There are no equals in the mind of someone chasing status, which means that the world will look like a never-ending arena of competition and envy.

Now, some will attempt to justify our playing of status games by claiming that it incentivizes people to create great things. That if we didn't shower people with money or recognition, they wouldn't go on to produce the technological and cultural advancements that make this world a better place.

While this may make sense at first glance, you'll realize just how flawed it is when you take a moment to sit with it.

If someone is incentivized by status to develop a technology, how plausible is it that the resulting product stems from the desire to increase the well-being of the world? Of course, that's what the innovator may claim, but deep inside, the selfish attachment to one's position will take precedence over everything.

Take social media for example. It's been widely reported that social media has had disastrous effects on the population's mental health, especially in our youth. If the people responsible for these tools were truly driven by the desire to create a better world, they would make sweeping reforms to ensure that their platforms never cause additional harm. But as you know, that rarely happens. Instead, they continue onward with their development, exploiting even more vulnerabilities in our psychology so they could maximize engagement and claim their place in the cultural zeit-geist. These people are not driven by the common good; they are driven by status.

The anthropologist Ernest Becker once wrote that we are "gods with anuses." What he meant was that humans are equipped with godlike imaginations that can compose beautiful music, build towering skylines, and even send rockets into space. But at the same time, the biological container that houses this incredible mind has been inherited from our monkey ancestors. It is a body that defecates, secretes, and deteriorates until it ceases to function. The tension between what we're capable of and what we've inherited is the core struggle of the human condition.

Status is one of those ugly things that we've inherited from our evolutionary ancestors, as the quest for dominance is seen throughout the animal kingdom. We all know this, yet our conditioning has convinced us to believe that it's a worthy pursuit. It tells us that if you play the game right, you'll get everything you desire. But of course, what you desire has also been planted by the game, ensuring that you'll never be able to leave.

The solution is to do away with status, and to choose compassion instead. Compassion is the ability to extend full presence to people, regardless of who they are or what they've achieved. It's to see that people are not defined by their proximity to your goals, but by the unity of the human experience. In the end, we all find our way to the soil or the sea, and that humbling fact makes you appreciate every person that accompanies you on this ride.

There are some that claim that viewing the world without the lens of status is impractical, and that you must play the game to achieve your goals. And to that I'd ask, "Who would you respect more: The person that strategically chooses who to appreciate, or the person that can do that for anyone?" The paradox of declining status is that there is a magnetism to it, and that manifests through the allocation of trust.

The people I admired most at the office weren't the charismatic leaders that knew how to close deals.

Rather, they were the few people that showed reverence for everyone, whether it was a potential client or the building custodian. They would know the names of all the cleaning staff and their family members, and would listen to them with the same presence they would have for their own boss. There were no motives to these dynamics other than being curious about the person in front of them, irrespective of who they were. That was my aspiration as well.

Krishnamurti said that "it is no measure of health to be well adjusted to a profoundly sick society." When you see that this sickness is caused by our justification of status, then you'll see just how healthy our relationships can be once you remove it. The immediate effect is that there's a full embrace of the person in front of you, and there's nothing you expect other than sharing that moment together. The long-term effect, which is even more profound, is that you start to embrace yourself without condition as well.

If the inner critic is a reflection of how you view others, then what happens when you no longer care about one's status? Well, then you stop using your own place in society to determine your self-worth. You understand the frivolity of it all, and see the utter hollowness of using achievement as a barometer for acceptance. You redirect any external attention back toward your inner compass, and use it as the primary force to guide you.

This is why self-understanding is a communal affair. If reflection is the principle that reveals why you think the way you do, then relationship is the principle that helps you put those revelations in action. There's a constant feedback loop between the self and the world, and this helps to refine your intuition over time.

But as you'll recall, there's one final principle to go over.

That's because as your intuition is refined, you learn so many lessons from each adjustment that is made. And what makes the self and the world feel fluid is when you share everything you've picked up along the way. By doing so, you dissolve the boundary between you and the other, and connect in a way that neither reason nor logic can quite explain.

The only way this happens is through the age-old principle of creation, which will reveal more about your capabilities than anything ever can.

CHAPTER 12
CREATE: THE EXPRESSION OF AGENCY

CREATIVITY IS NOT A LUXURY; it's a birthright. It's not something you do; it's something you are.

You will either nod in agreement to that statement, or you'll find it questionable. If you're skeptical about the claim, then it's usually for one reason: You've mistaken creativity for art.

When people don't think they're creative, they believe they lack the talent to emulate what is socially lauded. They'll see that what culture deems "creative" is a colorful painting, a resonant song, a timeless poem, a TV show, and so on. They'll look at these cultural artifacts and think, "I can't do that. I just work in some non-creative field and spend my leisure time doing non-creative things."

Well, as you're used to hearing by now, that is

conditioning. Anytime you use an external barometer to make an internal conclusion, you deny your intuition and restrict yourself. So the first step here is to understand what creativity is without any idea of what it's supposed to be.

At its core, creativity is the birthing of anything into existence. And crucially, it doesn't need to result in a tangible product that you can touch or see. Creativity is just as salient in an idea or concept as it is in a product or artifact. All that matters is that it originated from your body or mind.

Let's say that you spent the afternoon organizing your room. Most people wouldn't say that's a creative act, given that no new product came out of it. But it is. You created **order** as you moved the various objects in your room around, and did it in a way that felt intuitive. That is creativity.

Another example is a conversation with a friend. You are creating a sequence of words as you articulate your thoughts, which then go on to have the effect of creating insights and thoughts in your friend's mind. That would have never happened if you weren't there.

Our very existence ensures that we create in every moment. Our bodies and minds constantly dance between order and chaos, and it's the intricate movement between the two that constructs our shared reality.

So if you accept the premise that creativity is inherent to who we are, what would it take to actually *feel* that way? After all, it's one thing to accept the argument in theory, and another to truly believe it. I'm guessing that the next time you call your friend, you won't interpret it as anything more than a phone chat.

Well, there's a single word that makes all the difference. It's what will make a given action feel like it's imbued with creativity, regardless of what it is.

That word is **agency**.

Agency is when your actions are fully aligned with your interests, which makes those actions feel meaningful. Meaning is a close cousin of agency because when curiosity is leading the way, you approach your days with intention. And when you have intention in what you do, you begin to interpret your actions as an expression of creativity.

Let's take the example of you chatting with your friend to illustrate this.

Consider these two scenarios:

(A) You reach out to your friend to have a standard catch-up call,

(B) You invite your friend over to record a conversation about an epiphany you both had.

Scenario B will be viewed as a creative act in a way that Scenario A will not. That's because in Scenario B, there is an intention behind what you're both discussing, and there's a desire to encapsulate that moment so it can be revisited. Even though you're simply having a discussion in both scenarios, one discussion will be interpreted as a dance of dialogue whereas the other will be just another phone call. This is why podcasters are often referred to as creators while telemarketers never receive that reference. The level of agency that births a conversation is what frames it as an act of creativity.

When you embody this intention in what you do, two things happen. The first is that you stop questioning whether a creative act is worth doing. In the same way that a child plays without justification, you express without expectation. A child doesn't play because she'll be paid for it, and similarly, you don't create because you'll be praised for it. You do it for its own sake, which is the sentiment behind the adage that "a creative adult is a child who has survived."*

The second thing that happens is that you begin to feel how time dissolves. When you no longer doubt

---

* This quote is commonly misattributed to Ursula K. Le Guin, who has denied ever saying it. Regardless, it's a wonderful statement.

how you spend your attention, you understand what it feels like to be fully immersed in the moment. You have total conviction knowing that this is *exactly* what you're supposed to be doing, and this realization makes a mockery of the past and the future. The only thing on center stage is what you're currently working on, which turns worry and fear into peripheral characters in the theater of your mind.

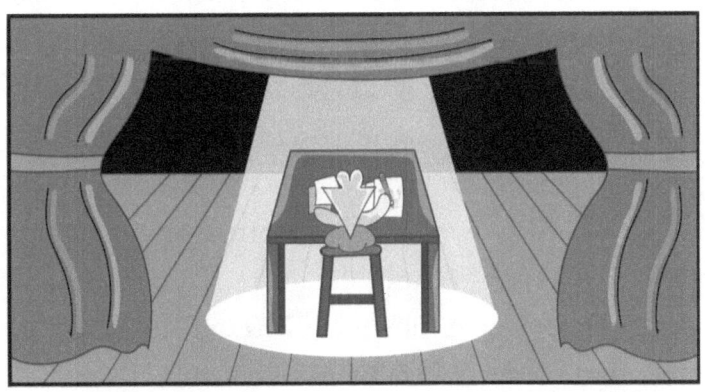

I know this because creativity saved me from my darkest moments. When I reflect back on my deepest points of suffering, it always stemmed from an inability to be present. I was either dwelling in the past by reliving a memory, or projecting a future by fearing an illusion. I was hiding in the corners of my imagination instead of basking in the light of the real.

Things started to change when I got serious about

making music in my spare time. Thanks to the encouragement of a few loved ones, I doubled down on learning how to make beats in an effort to express my lifelong interest in music. I had no audience for my work, but that was of little importance. What mattered was that I finally had a sense of agency over my life as I dedicated countless hours to actualizing whatever potential I believed I had. That belief in my own abilities was the first ray of light that bursted through the fog of my depression.

Not a day went by where I didn't practice my craft, as I knew that this was my conduit to accessing the present moment. And with each point of contact, I felt a wave of clarity wash over my worries, eroding them with each touch. As the days turned to months, I started experiencing something I hadn't felt in a long time: **contentment**. It felt foreign when I first noticed it, but what made it beautiful was the realization that it wasn't conditional. I wasn't feeling content because someone approved of my work or declared it a big achievement. I was content because I knew what it meant to finally be present, and that I could cultivate it on my own accord.

Creativity is the final principle of self-understanding because it's the greatest affirmation of what you're capable of. Every creative endeavor carries a texture of challenge because it requires you to learn, and learning is rarely easy. But because it is aligned with your true curiosities, you approach it with the agency required to imbue that challenge with meaning. And whenever a pursuit is meaningful, you ensure that you show up each day as the best version of yourself.

If reflection reveals who you are and relationship reveals the world you want to see, then creation is what merges those two domains together. By expressing the core of who you are through the medium of your choice, you act as a beacon for those that share a similar core as well. Creativity is a vehicle that you can drive according to your curiosities, and the best part is that it can hold the kind of passengers you'd love to be around.

But through it all, remember that creativity is an

avenue to knowing yourself. You can share its outcomes with others to build a sense of community, but the process itself must come from the commitment to stretch your capabilities. The essence of creation comes from a deep conviction in who you are, and not the desire to be embraced by the approving arms of conditioning.

This is a crucial point, which is why we'll unpack it further in the next chapter. And in doing so, you'll be conscious of when you're using creativity as a conduit to self-understanding, and when you might be using it to make up for a deficiency in self-worth.

CHAPTER 13
PURSUE MASTERY, NOT STATUS

IMAGINE that you're at a party where a friend shows a painting he made. This is surprising because nobody (including you) knew that he painted, and when you take a closer look at his work, your surprise grows into awe. It's the most beautiful thing you've seen, and everyone there agrees.

Now, there'll be two types of reactions your friend will receive:

1. A pleasant disbelief at the discovery of his talent,
2. A strong encouragement to post his work and sell it online.

We see this dynamic all the time, where people that reveal a "hidden" talent are then told to open up a store or start a business around it. A common way to compliment one's creativity is to suggest that they commodify it.

This is because for most people, a creative endeavor is a means to some end. It needs to result in views, in money, or in some form of recognition that amplifies its validity. It can't be an end in itself because there would be no way to determine how valuable it can be.

This is what creativity looks like through the lens of conditioning. It is only deemed worthwhile if other people say it is, and oftentimes, that value is made trackable through some metric. Influencers have followers, musicians have streams, writers have subscribers. And whenever a metric is introduced in this way, a status game is born.

Whenever you start an endeavor, there's no game to play because everything stems from your true curiosities. It's intrinsically driven so there's no benchmark to set it against. But after some time, the allure of validation turns your attention outward, causing you to compare yourself to the advertised successes of others. This leads to envy, fear, and similar emotions that only an external scorecard can conjure, all of which make you doubt what you're doing. Such are the consequences of drinking the poison of status.

Fortunately though, there is an antidote to this, and its name is mastery.

Mastery is the quest to improve yourself as an end in itself. Comparisons are not made with other people, but only with prior versions of yourself. You're not trying to become a better writer, musician, podcaster, etc. to improve your standing amongst others. Rather, you're doing it to prove to yourself that you can exercise your potential by contributing everything you can to actualize that untapped resource.

Status is obtained by collecting attention, whereas mastery is achieved by refining intuition. Status is always comparative, so external validation is a prerequisite to feeling secure. Mastery, on the other hand, is gauged by your unique sense of progress, which can only be derived from within.

By pursuing mastery, you march to the beat of your own drum, while ensuring that the quality of that drum continues to improve over time.

However, this leads to a contradiction.

How do you know that you're making progress without the validation of others? If you disregard external opinion, how can you tell that you're on the right track to mastery? Take the example of a writer who thinks he's God's gift to man, but no one ever reads his work. Self-confidence without credibility is often just another way of saying "delusional."

Well, those who pursue mastery may disregard the need for external validation, but they still accept the power of external *inspiration* to help guide their work. This difference is important. They don't need others to approve of what they're doing, but they will take the best of what others have offered to help shape their personal tastes and preferences.

Of all the assets one cultivates on the journey to mastery, the most important is intuition. Intuition provides you with the ability to discern between what's good, what's not, and what has the potential to break new ground... all without the need to listen to any crowd or tribe. It is the force that allows you to gauge your creative progress, all without the need to rely on external measurements to give you that sense of direction.

The best way to sharpen that intuition is to read,

watch, or listen to those that have already mastered their craft, and to update your model of mastery based on how you interpret their creations. If you earnestly hold yourself to a high enough standard, you won't be in a situation where you think you're on the right path when you've actually gone astray. The paradox of mastery is that even if you could care less about status, people will find their way to you since mastery is a gravitating force of its own.

The key here is to continue seeing status for the societal poison that it is, and to resist its allure.

Even if you don't consider yourself a creative person, I can't overstate the importance of creating *something* as a conduit to knowing yourself. As we went over in the last chapter, this is because creativity is an expression of agency, where your interests are in full alignment with your actions. It doesn't need to fulfill an external goal or milestone; all that matters is that you enjoy it and can feel time dissolve when you do. This ability to be present is the closest you'll get to the core of what moves you.

The next step is to layer on the pursuit of mastery. It doesn't mean that you need to become an expert at whatever you've chosen, but that you're committed to seeing what you're capable of. Instead of spending all your free time consuming things (like the majority of people do), you'll spend some of it creating and improving your craft. When you do this, you'll viscerally understand what it feels like to be working toward something that matters, which makes you believe in your potential. This belief in yourself is what strengthens your conviction, which increases your capacity to trust your intuition.

One practical way to actualize this is to create for just one hour each day. Identify that hour where you typically squander it to some streaming service, and use it to edify yourself. An hour works well because it's short enough to implement, yet long enough to encourage a flow state. Keep in mind that compounding isn't limited to finance; an hour of creativity each day can lead to astronomical results over time. The key is to continue cultivating the patience to show up each day, knowing that the fruits of your labor will arrive long after you've sown the seeds.

Finally, remember that creativity isn't limited to art; it's whatever you designate it to be. It's just as present in building relationships as it is in sitting down to work on a novel. It can be just as prevalent in an office as it is in a studio. What matters is that the endeavor has potential for continuous improvement, and that you're doing it because you truly want to. There is no incentive other than your curiosity and the desire to challenge yourself. Those are the only requisites when it comes to selecting a craft that will reveal what you're capable of.

Now, at this moment, you might be thinking:

"Okay, I understand the importance of creativity, but I'm not quite sure how the other principles connect. How do the threads of (1) reflection, (2) relationship, and (3) creativity tie together to form the basis of self-understanding? What does the dynamic between the three principles look like?"

That's a great question, and one that encourages a summary of sorts. So in the next (and final) chapter, we'll bring everything together in the form of a story that acts as an overview of it all.

CHAPTER 14
HIKING WITH THE INNER COMPASS

EVERY DAY we traverse the terrain of life.

It's an uphill terrain because our very existence is a fight against disorder. Our minds are distracted, our calendars are full, and our bodies are stressed. Life is a continuous chain of solving problems, which is why it feels more like a challenging hike than a casual stroll.

The beautiful thing, however, is that each of us has been gifted with an inner compass. This is a tool that helps us navigate this difficult terrain by indicating where to go given our values, interests, and curiosities. So while the trek may be arduous, there's a serenity that emerges from knowing that you're headed in the right direction.

By default, the inner compass is calibrated at true north. This is because presence is our baseline state, as we enter the world with the keen ability to disregard the past and the future. There's a contentment that arises from this reality, and that gives us the **conviction** to navigate existence in a way that feels intuitive.

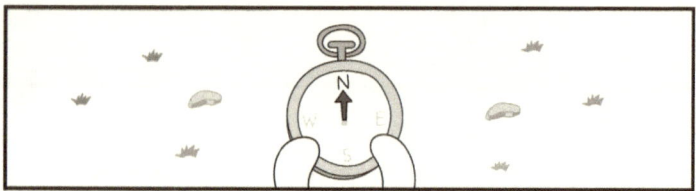

But things don't stay this way for very long.

The problem is that there are forces that actively sway us from true north, which are known as the winds of **conditioning**.

We are so easily swayed by these winds because they create the illusion of certainty. They take the form of social expectations, suggestions, and judgments that make you feel like everyone else has the answers. This causes you to fear and dampen your intuition, which will place you on a path that is not inherently yours.

And it's this misalignment that causes suffering to arise.

Sadly, many people continue down this route as a way to avoid uncertainty. They give up contentment so they could gain safety, and as a result, will rarely feel present. That's because when you know that you're living a lie, you can't help but to wonder what it'd be like to embody the truth.

At a certain point, however, you can no longer ignore this feeling. For some, it happens when they confront their mortality and know that something needs to change. For others, they're tired of feeling numb and understand that embracing the unknown is a way to reinvigorate their life.

Regardless of the scenario, one thing is driving their desire to recalibrate their inner compass. They can no longer ignore the pull of knowing themselves, which is embodied through a distant magnet that is pulling on the hands of their compass.

This is how the pursuit of self-understanding begins. It's one of the most worthwhile pursuits you'll ever take, which means it'll be challenging. So in an attempt to demystify this challenge, I introduced three principles that will help make it concrete.

The first principle is to **reflect**. It's to hit pause on your hike, to see where you've gone astray, and to know why that happened. The key is to remember that **wherever there's tension, there's a tale**, and the goal of reflection is to uncover the story that's driving any source of fear.

A reliable way to do this is through a regular journaling practice, where you try to detail *why* you're feeling these tensions. Journaling helps you release whatever you're feeling out onto the page, which gives you the space to examine the contents of your mind without being caught up in it. And if you do this for long enough, you'll uncover the conditioning that resides at the root of it all.

By clearly seeing how you've gone astray, your inner compass reveals something that was once obscured: a path that will ultimately lead you back to your true north.

Now that this path has been revealed, you can also be mindful of the manner in which you'll approach it. This clarity will be embedded in the second principle, which is to **relate**.

Society is a giant game that's governed by competition and envy. The reason you initially strayed from your conviction is because you adopted the rules of this game, all of which were crafted by other hands. These rules encourage you to rank people by their status, to view people by what they can offer, and to introduce conditions into your interactions. This made you listen to those with perceived authority, which served to undermine confidence in yourself.

But with the benefit of reflection, you now see a brighter path forward, and see the detriment of playing by these rules. You begin to understand that everyone can be candidates of deep appreciation, regardless of the benefits they can provide for you. You recognize the beauty in accepting people for who they are, which allows you to accept yourself without condition as well.

If **reflection** reveals your unconditioned path and **relationship** reveals the people that will accompany you, then **creativity** compels you to move forward on it. Since creativity is an act of expression, it's a kinetic force that propels you toward the person you're capable of becoming. This is further solidified by a commitment to mastery, which ensures that any point of comparison will be redirected from the outside to within.

Agency is of utmost importance in a creative act, and when you truly believe in what you're doing, you are attuned to the present moment. As the past and future dissipate, so do your doubts and fears. What remains is an inner compass that is properly aligned to true north, resulting in a mind that is free from the clutches of conditioning.

When you are in alignment with your intuition, there will be a fluidity that accompanies your days. By fluidity, I'm not referring to relaxation, as an uphill hike doesn't encourage that. What I mean by fluidity is that you know exactly what move to make, what step to take, and what obstacle to tackle without rationalizing your way through it. You'll know exactly what to do because you understand that the answer is already within.

However, it's only inevitable that this alignment will fall apart in some moments. Someone might say something to make you doubt yourself, an event may happen that makes you question everything, and so forth.

The winds of conditioning can return in full force when you least expect it, which may blow you off course once again.

The great thing, however, is you now know exactly how to get back on track.

Reflect to calibrate. **Relate** to connect. **Create** to express.

Place these three principles at the heart of your intentions whenever your core is shaken or disturbed. In doing so, you commit to trusting yourself, which has the effect of building up the magnet that keeps you aligned to true north.

The more you internalize the three principles, the stronger the magnet gets. So while the winds of conditioning will continue to blow, the effect they have on your hike will lessen. Since the magnet has a stronger field that keeps your compass aligned, the winds won't veer you off course as dramatically as they once did. What was once an upheaval will be a slight stumble as your conviction persists amidst the harsh conditions.

This ability to stay anchored is what will yield the courage to trust yourself. If you know who you truly are, then no opinion or outburst can take away from that self-understanding. The tragedy is that this wisdom tends to come into full bloom toward the end of life, which only gives you a few years to appreciate it. But by applying these principles now, you don't need to take decades of detours to stay on the path that you were uniquely meant to traverse.

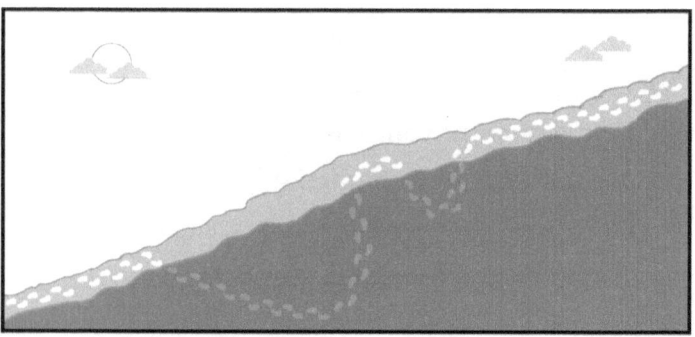

The great conundrum is that we go on this hike knowing that it ends. Once we reach the vantage point, that's it. There is no return trip, and yet we must continue onward.

What this means is that every step we take is precious, but we have to view it as such. When your landscape is fogged up by conditioning, you can't internalize the preciousness of each step because they don't feel like your steps. It feels like you're trudging on someone else's path, and that lack of agency prevents you from accessing the truth.

But when you seek to know yourself, everything changes. You see how your blend of interests, values, and curiosities is purely localized to your mind, and you realize how fortunate you are to be you. It's the resulting gratitude for existence that allows you to see how precious every step is.

This is how knowledge becomes understanding. You *know* that life is precious, but you *understand* it only when you dive deeper into who you are. The gap is bridged by committing to this pursuit, and by experiencing the labyrinth that is your own mind.

Every hike culminates in the same destination, so the question isn't about how it ends. Rather, the question is about how you'll feel once you reach it, and if you can survey the whole journey with a deep appreciation for how your inner compass has led you.

Because in the end, a well-lived life is a collection of moments that were imbued with presence. So by embracing who you are today, you're contributing to the peace you'll feel in that final moment where no more tomorrows remain.

POSTSCRIPT
THE ANTIDOTE TO ENVY

Writing reveals that a wiser version of yourself is available when you need that person the most. This is the sentiment that drives my desire to write, and everything I publish can be found on my blog, More To That.

Over the years, I've written (and illustrated) many stories and reflections. Each one is a snapshot of my thinking at a given time, which provides me with the benefit of revisiting them whenever I'd like. In the same way that photos capture personal memories, essays capture personal insights. So if you find yourself struggling with a problem you once addressed, you can go back and read the solution you once came up with as well.

Of the many pieces I've written, there's one I revisit whenever I get lost in the social comparison trap. It's called "The Antidote to Envy", and when I read it, I can feel my attention gravitate back toward the inner domain. The storm of envy subsides, and my mind is instantly refreshed about what matters in life.

So whenever you find yourself struggling with envy, feel free to flip forward to this postscript at any time. And if you then need a reminder of how to put self-understanding into practice, then flip back to the introduction and start this book once again. The human condition is timeless, and so are the principles that help you make the most of it.

Before I get into the piece, I want to first thank you for reading this book. Your attention is the most valuable thing you can provide, and I have done my best to write this book in a way that optimizes for it. With that said, if anything I've written has resonated with you, please send me a message at contact@moretothat.com. I love hearing from readers, and would love to know how your inner compass has guided you throughout your own hike as well.

In the meantime, there's one final postscript to share, and I hope that reading it will provide you with the same clarity I had while writing it. Enjoy.

THE ANTIDOTE TO ENVY

I recently came across a passage from Krishamurti's *Think On These Things* that gave me pause. I rarely highlight entire paragraphs when I read, but this one was so poignant that I had to elevate it from the page and into my memory.

Here it is:

> *I am envious because I want to be as beautiful as you are; I want to have the fine clothes, the elegant house, the high position that you have. Being dissatisfied with what I am, I want to be like you; but, if I understood my dissatisfaction and its cause, then I would not want to be like you or long for the things that you have.*

In other words, if once I begin to under-
stand what I am, then I shall never compare
myself with another or be envious of anyone.
Envy arises because I want to change myself
and become like somebody else. But if I say,
"Whatever I am, **that** *I want to under-*
stand," then envy is gone; then there is no
need of discipline, and out of the under-
standing of what I am comes integration.

I've since re-read this passage many times, and there's one sentence that continues to capture my attention:

   Whatever I am, **that** *I want to understand.*

Today, I want to talk about what it means to know yourself, and how this results in the elimination of envy.

I'd like to start with an observation: Some people are open about their struggles with envy, while the majority hide it. I'm calling it an observation because I can't point to a research paper that clearly shows this asymmetry, yet my personal exploration of human nature indicates that this is likely true.

Simply put, envy is one of those complicated

emotions that hasn't had its time in the spotlight yet. Vulnerability came on center stage when Brené Brown gave a popular TED Talk on it, while depression has emerged as something that's okay to discuss in recent years. Envy, however, hasn't quite found that comfort zone. Revealing that you're an envious person won't yield much sympathy, and is often accompanied by a sense of shame that you feel this way.

But envy is one of the most pervasive problems in today's world, especially as social media normalizes the successes of others, making you feel like you're "under-performing" the average when in reality you're being shown a highlight reel of outliers. You're always comparing yourself to someone ahead of you, and the goalpost will keep moving because the algorithm ensures that it moves on your behalf. And whenever a hierarchy like this exists, the fingers of envy creep within.

All this results in a conundrum. Envy is running through everyone's veins, yet no one feels like they could talk about it. No one wants to admit that the success of others makes them feel inadequate, and that this inadequacy dampens their sense of self-worth. Not only is it difficult to admit this to others, but it's just as hard to admit it to oneself.

But that last word—*oneself*—is where the solution to this resides.

Ultimately, envy is the result of not knowing who you are. It arises when you outsource your definitions of success to whatever norms you've adopted— whether consciously or not. In one person's case, it might be wealth. In another, it may be social media followers. In another, it could be the size of a home. Regardless of what the barometer is, the fact that you desire it means that you're looking beyond the contents of your mind and into the collective pool of society. You're ceasing to look into what makes you uniquely you, and are gazing into the chaos of chasing that which you don't understand.

One of my favorite Joker lines from *The Dark Knight* is when he says that people are like dogs chasing cars; they won't know what to do if they actually catch them. I find that the same thing applies to the chase of success or anything that might make you feel envious. If you got the thing that was the subject of your envy, then what? Is that it? Are you satisfied?

Chances are, you'll be like the dog having caught the car. There's simply nothing you could do, except one of two things:

1. Keep yourself busy by chasing another car, or
2. Learn that this entire chase is pointless.

#1 is what psychologists refer to as the hedonic treadmill, while #2 is what I refer to as the antidote to envy.

There is an interesting thing that happens when you see how society is organized into a giant game. You see the puppet strings of incentives and the invisible hierarchies that govern the way the pieces move, and this realization is both fascinating and disconcerting. No human being wants to be reduced to an algorithm, but it's funny how if you get enough of us together, we behave in ways that are just as predictable as the execution of a file.

To see beyond the game is to direct your attention inward instead. Rather than chasing the next car, you'll explore why you wanted to chase that car in the first place. Because if you explore your own mind's motives in great detail, you'll learn more about humankind than playing any game ever will.

> *Whatever I am, **that** I want to understand.*

The reason why self-understanding leads to the

elimination of envy is because when you explore the maze of your mind, you simply have no room to want what another person has. There are more mysteries within the bounds of your own life than any novel can ever express, and this journey will take an entire lifetime to cover.

Remember: You didn't choose your genes, your parents, your upbringing, your interests. Pretty much everything of consequence is the result of happenstance, and that is where we all begin. We're equipped with a mind and body that we didn't choose, yet the temptation is to believe that we know who we are. Nothing could be further from the truth, and the way to get closer to this truth is not to compare yourself to another, but to know what "yourself" even means in the first place.

At its core, self-understanding is a commitment to figuring out why you think the way you think. In my case, writing these kinds of essays is my way of understanding myself. I don't do it to build an audience or to seek recognition for them. I do it because I want to explore why I struggle with the things I struggle with, and why I love the things I love. Given that I wasn't the conscious agent that constructed my mind, it's up to me to figure out what's really going on underneath the hood of it all. No one can do that for me but me, and no one can do that for you but you.

Envy is inversely correlated with self-examination. The less you know yourself, the more you look to others to get an idea of your worth. But the more you delve into who you are, the less you seek from others, and the dissolution of envy begins.

ACKNOWLEDGMENTS

Life is made whole through a connection with other lives. Writing this book helped me realize just how true that statement is, and how fortunate I am to be supported by the people that have been present throughout it.

To Seong Ho Yeo and Hee Sook Moon, who show me what resilience and love are capable of accomplishing.

To Joannza Lo, whose love and support gives me faith that the uncertainties of life are worth navigating.

To Maya Yeo, who reminds me of what it means to follow your inner compass without fear.

To Eugene Yeo, who reliably shows up and commits to progressing forward.

To Brian Jong, who helped me see how creativity can reinvigorate a friendship for decades to come.

To Nam Bui, who continually uses kindness and humor as a vehicle for connection.

To Jason Yeh, who helped me regain my footing with a gift that I will always remember.

To Jeannie Wakamatsu, who has been there since the beginning and helped me navigate the complexities of early adulthood.

To Jennifer Skillman, for guiding me through some of my darkest moments and acting as a light through it all.

To Michael Gomes, Luis Sandoval, and Jason Phan, who create an atmosphere of humor while also building a foundation of support.

To Felix Yeh and Andy Chen, for being just one phone call away.

To the Yeo and Moon families, who have transcended distances to accept me.

To the Lo and Lam families, who have embraced me as one of your own.

To all my creator friends, who have supported me throughout the journey of discovery and expression. I hope I've been able to do that for you as well.

To anyone who has read, viewed, or shared my work: Thank you. I'm filled with gratitude that you've dedicated some of your attention to my ideas. It's a privilege to be able to share space with you in this way.